T0392285

The
Babylon
Line

The
Babylon
Line

Richard Greenberg

A PLUME BOOK

PLUME
An imprint of Penguin Random House LLC
375 Hudson Street
New York, New York 10014

Copyright © 2016 by Richard Greenberg

P REGISTERED TRADEMARK—MARCA REGISTRADA

Library of Congress Cataloging-in-Publication Data

Names: Greenberg, Richard, 1958– author.
Title: The Babylon Line : a play / by Richard Greenberg.
Description: New York : Plume, [2016]
Identifiers: LCCN 2016029989 (print) | LCCN 2016037459 (ebook) |
    ISBN 9780399576553 (paperback) | ISBN 9780399576560 (ebook)
Subjects: | BISAC: PERFORMING ARTS / Theater / General. | PERFORMING ARTS /
    General. | PERFORMING ARTS / Theater / Playwriting.
Classification: LCC PS3557.R3789 B33 2016 (print) | LCC PS3557.R3789 (ebook)
    | DDC 812/.54—dc23
LC record available at https://lccn.loc.gov/2016029989

147204767

Characters

AARON PORT

JOAN DELLAMOND

FRIEDA COHEN

ANNA CANTOR

MIDGE BRAVERMAN

JACK HASSENPFLUG

MARC ADAMS

MR. LEVITT

JAY BECKERHOFF

JOAN'S HUSBAND

MIDGE'S HUSBAND

WOMAN AT COOKOUT

PRINCIPAL

GUY AT PARTY   AS CAST

MIMI X

THERESA

SYDELLE BOSTWICK

RHONDA HAGENBRUCH

ABE

RUTHIE

LENORE

BRIAN COHEN

TODD COHEN

RAMONA

Act One

AARON: The End.

   . . .

By which I mean what exactly?

Once, briefly, I loved someone who hated quotations: She claimed they'd ruined her life.

Nevertheless:

"Death sanctions all stories," wrote Walter Benjamin.

But does it?

And even if it does,

the end that comes with death is by definition

someone else's

and so can't really bring us close to the notion. And for a lapsed atheist like me—by which I mean, I continue to believe there is no God but suspect for me He might make an exception—even that final ending is, possibly, not so final.

   . . .

But this is no kind of introduction. All right, then:

The year is 2016 and I am eighty-seven years old. I look wonderful.

So much has turned out nicely.

. . .

And that's about that for 2016. Listen:

There's a story I've been meaning to tell and, I guess, avoiding for a long time.

It's a simple story about a few events

that took place in late fall and early winter forty-nine years ago,

and I may not come off well in it.

But

if not now—when? So.

Okay:

The year is 1967 and I am thirty-eight years old. I look fretful.

So much has turned out badly.

Lights on a high school classroom.
Night.

Aaron is with Frieda and Anna.

FRIEDA: We wanted, Anna and I, to take Contemporary Events and Politics, but that sold out like a shot when they announced that Dr. Rose Franzblau might be a Guest Speaker,

which I hear

is not the case—

So back to registration and they ask us if we'd like to take Flower Arranging, instead. It's taught by John Scorfutto?

You know,

he owns Hempstead Turnpike Bloomery? (Oh, that's right, you're not from here.) Well, I never use them.

Everything there is carnations; so cheap. Anyway, when it comes to Flower Arranging I think I'm more of an expert than John Scorfutto.

Whereas Anna, whenever she's tried, her flowers come out looking like gloves that nobody's wearing. So, no, thank you to Flower Arranging, and they wonder, can we do Wednesdays?

As it happens, we can and writing was available so here we are.

ANNA: Actually, for me there was more to it than that. I've always been a good writer.

I won a writing award in high school.

FRIEDA: Which was before they invented the pencil. You didn't have a dirty fingernail; you had to recite from memory.

No, I'm kidding.

However, my question is:

Will we be, in this class, expected actually to write?

AARON: It's a writing class.

FRIEDA: Uh-huh.

Now, that perturbs me a little.

AARON: Don't let it.

FRIEDA: I'm no James Michener.

AARON: I should hope not.

FRIEDA: I'm not claiming to be James Michener.

ANNA: Can we write about current affairs?

AARON: You may.

ANNA: Because that was the class we wanted to take.

AARON: I believe I knew that.

ANNA: Though this is exciting, too.

FRIEDA: But we haven't been formally introduced: I'm Frieda Cohen.

You may have seen my house on the way over. It's the one with the well-known garden:

If you haven't seen it in person, it was featured in *Newsday*.

My husband, Lou, is a chemist and I have two boys.

Todd is nineteen, Brian is seventeen—they're the joy of my life.

And now let me introduce you to one of the most magnificent people you're ever going to meet:

This is Anna Cantor,

who, for whatever reason, got started late in the childbearing game

and has two adorable five-year-olds, Seth and Abby, who are twins!

ANNA: You don't have to tell him they're twins.

What? I have two five-year-olds who *aren't* twins?

FRIEDA: I was just pointing out—

ANNA (TO AARON): Twins are a lot more common than is generally known.

Midge enters.

FRIEDA: Midge! I didn't know you were taking this class!

MIDGE: French Cooking was full.

FRIEDA: Anna, you know Midge—from the Sisterhood.

ANNA: I've known her twenty years; you introduce us every time we meet. Hi, Midge. You look terrific!

MIDGE: Vitamin E.

FRIEDA: Mr. Port, this is another uncommonly superb person— Midge Braverman. Her husband is a CPA. Her son is, what, fifteen? Michael. And her other son, Stewart, is a year or so older.

AARON: Nice to meet you.

MIDGE (RE: AARON): He's a baby!

FRIEDA: Only comparatively—

AARON: I'm a lot older than I—

MIDGE: *This* is going to teach us to write?

AARON: I hope so—

Jack Hassenpflug enters, finds a seat.

FRIEDA: This gentleman I don't know; you're on your own with him.

AARON: If you'll excuse me. I have to . . .

He heads for his desk.

Marc Adams enters, pauses in doorway, tentative.

FRIEDA: Oh my God—I don't believe it.

MIDGE: Who is that?

ANNA: Marge Adams's boy, Marc.

FRIEDA: It's such a pity.

MIDGE: Which is Marge Adams?

FRIEDA: You'd only know her from the PTA, but she was before your time.

MIDGE: She's not Sisterhood?

FRIEDA: Marge *Adams*?

ANNA: He's not right, this Marc.

FRIEDA: He's not right in the head. He had so much promise.

ANNA: A sports star.

FRIEDA: A bully, though, kind of a mean kid—

MIDGE: What happened?

8

ANNA AND FRIEDA: Drugs.

MIDGE: Ooohh. What drugs?

ANNA: Dope.

FRIEDA: And marijuana.

MIDGE (GETTING IT): He was a user.

ANNA: This brilliant kid, isn't that terrible?

FRIEDA: On course to be valedictorian.

ANNA: Now all he does is take long walks and smile at everybody.

FRIEDA: Hello, he says. "Hello! Hello!"

ANNA: It's—the loss—

FRIEDA: The loss.

    Marc sees them.

MARC: Hello! Hello!

    He finds a seat.

ANNA: In a way, he's pleasant.

MIDGE: Such a shame.

ANNA: It happens.

MIDGE: These times.

FRIEDA: And he's taking this class. *Guttenyu.*

They take desks.

AARON: I guess we can start. Hello. Good evening. Welcome.
This is, as you know, Creative Writing.
I'm your instructor. My name is Aaron Port.
Uh, first: Don't feel you need to interpret the course title too rigidly. Any kind of writing is welcome: Fiction. Biography. Recipes.
Well, maybe not recipes.
What I mean to say is, this is not a highly formalized class. That doesn't seem appropriate to adult ed.
Anyway, that's not how I like to learn, so it won't be how I, um, teach.
I like to learn things obliquely. Watchcries, dogma, interest me less.
The way this will work is you will write, we will read, comment. Little by little, knowledge will accrue.
Hemingway, whatever we may think of him, wrote: "Write the truest sentence you know." Or something like that. I haven't memorized it verbatim.
I don't really like Hemingway much; he always sounds to me like a first-grade primer: Dick, Jane, and Ernie.

No one laughs.

But the true sentence . . . I that, I stand by that. All right.

Okay. Oh, by the way, I'm sorry but no smoking—I have asthma. So then.

You were asked to bring to this first class a sample of your writing, a little autobiographical something or . . .

along those lines.

Who would like to read first?

Silence and abashed expressions.

Shall I pick someone?

More deeply abashed expressions.

Has anyone brought anything?

Silence.

Okay, then.

Joan rushes in.

JOAN: Am I late?

> *They take her in. The three ladies look at one another*
> *with an opinion.*

AARON: A little, but—

JOAN: I'm so sorry—

AARON: You've missed very little. You are Mrs., um . . . (CONSULTS PAGE)

JOAN: Joan.

AARON: Dellamond, is it?

JOAN: I'll just sit here in the back.

She does.

AARON (A BIT THROWN BY HER): We were saying—write the truest thing you know. Hemingway . . . wrote, um . . .

Beat.

Have *you* brought anything to read?

JOAN: Oh God, no.

Subtle lights and Aaron talks to us.

AARON: And so:
A forty-five minute vamp.
A general discussion of important topics in literature ensues.
Mrs. Cohen, Mrs. Cantor, and Mrs. Braverman become quite heated debating Norman Mailer on David Susskind the other night and the possibility that Truman Capote is a homosexual.
Ganug.

To the class:

Since no one has brought in anything, I'm going to end early, but I do ask that next week you come with something.
Anything.
A paragraph.
As I said, there are no restrictions. I'm
. . .
. . .
. . .

very excited about your potential.
Good night.

The class starts to leave.

In the back of the room, Joan remains.

*Aaron sits at his desk, takes out a paperback, and starts
to read it. Then he notices Joan.*

AARON: May I help you?

JOAN: No.

> *Beat.*

AARON: Is there something—

JOAN: I'm waiting for the ladies to disperse. They're in the parking
lot now ripping you to shreds, I'd imagine
—but cheerfully!—
and I'm waiting for them to be gone.

AARON (NODS): Oh.

> *Beat.*

> Why?

JOAN: I don't like being shunned.

AARON: Do they shun you?

JOAN: They do.
Well, not *these*, I've just met these, but . . . their ilk.

Beat.

You don't have to stay with me—or do you have to lock up?

AARON: My train isn't for another . . .

JOAN: Oh, I see.

AARON: Wantagh Station has few amenities this time of night.

JOAN: No.
And in daylight it's even worse.

AARON: Usually when I come it's dusk.

JOAN: Dusk is a little better.

AARON: There's a—

JOAN (OVERLAPS): Dusk is—

AARON: —clemency to it—

JOAN (OVERLAPS): —nature's candlelight.

AARON: Yes!

JOAN: Tricky, tricky dusk.

Beat.

So you do the reverse commute?

AARON: I do.

JOAN: My husband is a regular commuter.

AARON: Ah.

JOAN: Works in the city; doesn't work at home.

AARON: That's more standard.

JOAN: Levittown is not where people generally come seeking opportunities.

AARON: No.

JOAN: There have been no gold rushes in Levittown. No one, to my knowledge, auditions here.

AARON: A bedroom community.

JOAN: People do sleep here. I can attest to that.
    . . .
    If that should be necessary. For any reason.

    Smiles awkwardly.

    He smiles awkwardly back.

    One would imagine that a person
    who lives in the city and works in Levittown would be involved in some singular pursuit.

    He shrugs, smiles, conceding.

Or is a failure . . . ?
A failure of some kind . . . ?

AARON (AMUSED?): Why do the ladies shun you?

JOAN: Well, I don't know that's the word.

AARON: It's your own word.

JOAN: They don't really *shun*—not in a formal,
not in a *lit*eral way.
. . .
No one's Amish.

AARON: Ha.

JOAN: Maybe it's me. Maybe I'm a paranoiac.
I haven't really made friends yet in Levittown.

AARON: It can take a while.
How long have you lived here?

JOAN: Eighteen years.

Beat.

AARON: That's a long time, eighteen years.

JOAN (VAGUELY): Yes.

Beat.

Why do you have to travel so far to teach?

AARON (TOO QUICKLY): Oh, I'm not a teacher! I mean
. . .
    a friend knew of this job and so—

JOAN: Yes, I think I know what you mean. Well.
    I wish you luck.

AARON: You are coming back?

    Backing off:

    Under six people, they can make us disband.

JOAN: I expect I'll try . . . to try again. Even so, I wish you luck.

    Lights.

    The following week.

JACK HASSENPFLUG: I fought in the Battle of Overloon. It was a big mess.
    There was a lot of death and bloodshed, including my friends, some of them.
    I was badly injured—but kept going.
    I still dream of it sometimes and I guess I wake up screaming because my wife is looking up at me and she says, "That again?"

    He's finished.

    The others are waiting for more. He realizes it.

    The End.

AARON: Thank you, Mr. Hassenpflug. Very . . . *Thank you.* Comments?

JACK: I don't wanna talk about it.

AARON: We don't have to.

JACK: I just wanted to get it down. That's all.

    Pause.

    Somebody else can read theirs now. Is that okay?

AARON: Um—

JACK: I just, uh, please?

AARON: All rightee . . .
    Does anyone . . . else . . . have

    Midge is making reluctant assenting faces.

    Mrs., um . . .

MIDGE: Braverman.

AARON (OVERLAPS): Mrs. Braverman, yes—have you—

MIDGE: I *do* have something.
    The thing is, I'm not really a writer. I meant to take French Cooking—

AARON: —and I'm sure you're not really a cook either; the difference is what you've written can't make us vomit: So . . . Please. Be brave.

MIDGE: . . . It's very short.

AARON: That's fine.

MIDGE: It's kind of . . . autobiographical? It's a *vignette*, really—

AARON: If you'd . . . read . . . ?

> *Midge nods. She reads.*

MIDGE: This happened twenty years ago.
> I was new in Levittown. So was Levittown. I was sitting on the lawn in a lawn chair.
> A middle-aged man walked by.

> *Lights shift slightly.*

> *Middle-aged man walks by.*

MAN: Your lawn.

MIDGE: Pardon?

MAN: Untended.

MIDGE: Mr. Levitt!
> What an honor to meet—

LEVITT: Excuse me.

> *He whips out a tape measure, kneels, measures the height of her lawn. Shows her the results.*

> Won't do.

19

MIDGE: My husband's had a summer flu.

LEVITT: There are local boys you can pay a quarter. You have arms.

He leaves.

MIDGE: So I got out the lawn mower—and do you know I mowed the lawn? I very much enjoyed it and felt pride when I looked at my newly mown lawn. And in a way, it changed my life because ever since, when I've felt stress or strain, I've mowed my lawn and it's calmed me down, in the warm-weather months. The End.

AARON: Thank you. Comments?

No one wants to. They look at one another, passing the buck. After a moment:

FRIEDA: What an SOB that Levitt was, wasn't he?

A various reaction.

You'd be sitting in your house, *which* you were paying for, suddenly he'd drive up in his limo and critique the rust on your mailbox or whatever.

I mean, I got along with him fine, but who was he, this *macher*? Treating us like we're inmates at his stalag?

ANNA: He could be very authoritarian, that's true.

FRIEDA: The man was a de*velo*per. That's not a person you respect.

So, what, we're supposed to be impressed at long last he builds a development where he would have permitted himself to live? 'Cause, believe me, in his others: no Jews.

Not that he'd be caught dead living here, this millionaire big shot.

I just didn't care for the man's *att*itude.

Beat.

AARON: That's interesting, Mrs., um, Cohen, but . . .

any comments on Mrs., uh, Braverman's story specifically?

FRIEDA: Oh.

Very nice, Midge.

Wonderful local color.

Silence.

AARON: Anyone else?

I see.

No one.

Well, then, any other writing?

Scans the room.

AARON: Mr., um, Adams, is it?

MARC: Marc.

AARON: Marc—

Have you anything?

MARC: I'm working.

AARON: Anything to *show* yet?

MARC: I'm working on something.

AARON: So . . . then . . . nothing.

MARC: Someday, yeah.

AARON: Okay.

MARC: Yeah.

AARON: Okay.

MARC: Yeah.

AARON: All right.

MARC: Yeah.

    Beat.

AARON: Well—

MARC: It's a magnum opus.

AARON: I'm sorry?

MARC: I'm working on a magnum opus.

AARON: Oh!

MARC: Yeah, it's a magnum opus. Six hundred, seven hundred pages—

AARON: I'm speechless.

MARC: Yeah, it's gonna be seven hundred, eight hundred pages—it's a magnum opus.

AARON: Well, we don't expect you to bring nor could we accommodate the whole, um, magnum o—

MARC: It's gonna be a thousand pages.

AARON: As you say: but. We'd love it if you'd show us an extract. Even a paragraph.

MARC: Yeah.

Beat.

When I have a paragraph, I'll bring it in.

AARON: That will be, um, splendid. So.

And now to us:

With nothing left to read, the floor is once again open to General Discussion.

Today's topic: The recent appearance on *Johnny Carson* of Gore Vidal, who, says Mrs. Cohen, is an acknowledged homosexual and, adds Mrs. Cantor, is related in some way no one can figure out to Jackie Kennedy but, claims Mrs. Braverman, loathes Truman Capote, which, asserts Mrs. Cohen, means nothing because why should they all like each other? to which Mrs. Cantor adds, Who knows? Maybe they had a thing, although, Mrs. Cantor further stipulates, her brother-in-law, Bunny, claims he, Bunny, heard a rumor that Capote really goes for the women, his effeminate mannerisms being merely a method of shielding himself from their potential onslaught anyway (Mrs. Cantor says Bunny continued), people in the know say he (Capote) is always having *lunch* with women, at which point, prematurely, I interject:

I see our time is up.

General reaction from the class. Start of leave-taking.

MIDGE: Jahn's for strawberry milk shakes?

ANNA: Sure.

FRIEDA: You go ahead, I'll join you there. I need to talk to Mr. Port a minute.

MIDGE: Okay.

Midge and Anna leave.

Joan loiters as far in the background as she can.

FRIEDA: Mr. Port?

AARON: Yes, Mrs., um—

FRIEDA: I'm wondering if you have any suggestions for me.

AARON: About . . . ?

FRIEDA: My writing.

AARON: Umm . . . You haven't written anything yet.

FRIEDA: Well, *that's* what I'm saying.

The thing is this: I have an extremely strong point of view, everyone would tell you that. What I don't have is a topic.

AARON: I don't like to assign topics.

FRIEDA: That's one of the problems I have with you.

AARON: What I'm wondering, Mrs., um, is, if you—Cohen—don't have a topic, about what is it that you have this very strong point of view.

FRIEDA: Whatever happens to happen. Listen, Mr. Port, I'm not asking you to pay my mortgage here, I would just like a suggestion as to a topic I could write about.

AARON: Well, of course, there's the commonest advice about writing—I've avoided it because it's so popular—but: Write what you know.

    Beat.

FRIEDA: Do you have any other suggestions?

AARON: . . . Um . . . No.

    She looks at him.

AARON: All right.
    . . . Write about what shames you.

FRIEDA: I can't do that.

AARON: We all put up resistance when it—

FRIEDA: I'm without shame.

Beat.

AARON: No one is without shame.

FRIEDA: Oh: These are *life* lessons?

AARON: Inevitably.

FRIEDA: The older instruct the younger in life.

AARON: Not always.

FRIEDA: Shame—sorry—I don't have it on tap . . .

AARON: Okay . . . Then . . . what scares you?

FRIEDA: Most often, I am the cause of fear in others. Not the other way around.

AARON: Shameless and fearless.

FRIEDA: What can I tell you, Mr. Port? I'm a conqueror.

AARON: Then write about that.

FRIEDA: And will you mock me, if I do?

AARON: Of course not.

FRIEDA: Yes, well.

I'll think about it.

Because I refuse to come up short here—I *never* come up short.

Notices Joan.

Oh, Mrs. Dellamond—you're still here.

JOAN: Uh, yes.

FRIEDA: Tell me, I've been wondering—do you actually live in Levittown?

JOAN: . . . Yes.

FRIEDA: Because I don't believe I've even *seen* you before this class. Not at functions.

Not at Henshaw's or Jahn's or TSS or ShopRite or the garden outlet.

JOAN: I . . . read a lot.

Beat.

FRIEDA: I see.

So you're *new* here?

JOAN: No.

FRIEDA: . . . I see.

The ladies and I are off to Jahn's for strawberry milk shakes. Would you care to join us?

JOAN: I

would

of course

and thank you so much but

I

need to speak with Mr. Port about something.

FRIEDA: Oh, do you?

Turns to Aaron.

Do you?

Back to Joan:

Another time, then.

She exits.

A moment. Aaron and Joan wait until she is out of earshot.

AARON: That wasn't a shunning, it didn't seem. That was *wel*coming.

JOAN: You have to beard the animal before you can go in for the kill.

AARON: Ah.

JOAN: Why do you have this job?

AARON: I . . . find it interesting to—

Doesn't believe it himself.

Fifteen bucks a week after you deduct transportation.

She smiles.

Even artists work for money, you know, though the idea constantly stuns them.

JOAN: Because I read a story you wrote.

AARON: . . . How?

JOAN: I went to the library and looked you up in the *Readers' Guide to Periodical Literature*—you only have one listing—

AARON: They're thorough in the *Readers' Guide* to—

JOAN: Then I requested the magazine with your story in it—they didn't have it, of course—so I went to the library in East Meadow, which is a much better library, and they had it on microfilm, so I read it.

AARON: How does it read on microfilm?

JOAN: Very well. I liked it!
Very tender and promising.

AARON: Oh God: *promising*—

JOAN: I would like to read more.

AARON: Soon.
   . . .
I'm trying to decide if I've been spied on.

JOAN: Researched.

AARON: Ah, researched.

JOAN: You interest me.

. . .

Backing off:

I wanted to see what I was getting for my . . . money. Fee.

AARON: Microfilm—very Double O Seven.

JOAN: This seemed the best way.

AARON: Yes; very practical.

JOAN: I'm a very practical woman.
A very realistic,
even a down-to-earth woman.

Beat.

Although my house is haunted.

Aaron laughs.

You may laugh, but it's true.

AARON: You have a ghost . . .

JOAN: I do—

AARON: Mucking about with things; tossing things ar—

JOAN: No, my ghost returns things to their proper places.

Things you're sure you left scattered about turn up neatly folded

in the drawers where they're meant to stay. I have a very fastidious ghost.

You don't believe me.

AARON: It's impossible.

JOAN: Why?

Beat. A bold decision:

AARON: I'm an atheist.

JOAN (LIGHTLY MOCKING): Oooh, I'm so scared.

And when did this atheism befall you?

AARON: I've been, um, considering it . . . for quite some— There are books—philosophers—

historians of religion—I've been—reading—finally,

you see where God came from the Paleolithic

superstitions, the ignorance that fueled it. And the terror that sustains it.

And there's no choice.

JOAN: And do you find that without God

literature is reduced to the mundane and deprived of poetry?

And is that why you're blocked?

AARON: I'm . . . not blocked.

JOAN: Are you not blocked?

AARON: . . . No.

JOAN: Oh, I thought you were.
      Well, as an atheist, shouldn't you be?

AARON: Why should that block me?

JOAN: Because there's no fate, no mystery;
      perversities are merely . . . perverse,
      not part of some as-yet-unrevealed pattern.
      All that's left are biology and social arrangements
      and they're better described by other disciplines.

AARON: There is . . . poetry without—truly; there *is*.

JOAN: What kind?

AARON: The poetry of
      . . . the accidental . . .

JOAN: Hmm.
      Hmm.
      I suppose that's deep.

      She notices his book.

      But you're reading.
      I don't want to distract you from your reading. What are you reading?

AARON: *Contempt.*

JOAN: Moravia?

AARON: Yes.

JOAN: I liked *Boredom*.

AARON: I did, too.

JOAN: I'm fond of novels that transport you to places where you're glad you're not. So much easier coming to the *end* of those.
Do you like Colette?

AARON: Never read her.

JOAN: Are you a *cave*man?
No wonder you don't believe in God, you're still worshipping *fire*. You *have* to read Colette.

AARON: Girls do.

JOAN: I am buying you a copy, I'm giving you an assignment.
We'll discuss it at Jahn's over strawberry milk shakes the color of Pepto-Bismol. They'll be our Left Bank, and our absinthe.

AARON: Okay.

JOAN: When?

AARON: Get me the book, I'm a fast reader.

JOAN: . . .
Well, all right.

AARON: Absolutely.

JOAN: Oh, how good!
      What a good thing that will be!

AARON: . . . Yes.

      Pause.

      Why are *you* here?

JOAN: . . . I'm
      . . . hiding out from the—

AARON: No—not here, in this room, now. Here—in this
      town, in this life.

JOAN: Oh—

AARON: There's a way people live here. You don't seem to—

JOAN: No.
      I don't.

      A moment.

      You live in the Village, don't—

AARON: Yes—

JOAN: It said so in the author description, but that was old—

AARON: Things haven't much changed—

JOAN: I lived there, too, twenty years ago.

That's where I met . . . my husband.

AARON: What were you doing *there*?

JOAN (WIDE-EYED): I had no idea!

I must have *wanted* something. Yes, that was it.

I wanted something. And I was pretty, then, believe it or—

AARON: Oh please.

JOAN: Yes, you're right, that was disingenuous—

A pretty girl

in those days in that place

could get in anywhere she wanted to go—

I guess that's still true—

and I wanted to be among the terrifying artists, I guess—so I *was* among the terrifying artists.

And I met my husband—only he wasn't an artist, which was so refreshing! He was an inventor;

well, at least he took out a lot of patents, and he was very handsome.

And we started

going around together—

Is this *nostalgie de la boue* starting to cloy?

AARON: I've got time to kill—

JOAN: Well.

We went to parties

that seemed ordinary at the time but turned out to be famous!

Chronicles of these parties have been widely published—we've been named in the lists of attendees—

although we go by an alias in these lists; we're known as "and many others."

AARON: That's my alias, too!

JOAN: I sensed we had things in common.

AARON: A natural affinity.

JOAN: One night
    —no, this is writing class, let me— Once upon a night—

AARON: Oh God.

JOAN: Once upon a very *hot July* night
    we found ourselves in a very small room among very many sweaty people
    and decided to go outside
    for a cigarette and a breath of air.
    Well, there wasn't a breath of air to be had on all Manhattan Island,
    so we settled for the smoke. We were on a pier—
    and dusk started,
    with the sky going the summer shades and his face looked at me
    this gorgeous, beseeching, adobe-colored face,
    and God knows what I could have been thinking, but I cried out: "I have so much hope!"
    And he said:

"The thing with feathers."

And, you see, this is where it's dangerous to be ignorant; the moral of this story is, "Be well read,"

because *I thought he'd made that up.*

Imagine my shock and consternation when I finally applied myself to Emily Dickinson. Because I cannot tell you how many years of dinners I'd endured during which we discussed the green beans, lengthily, and I'd assure myself: No, no, this is the man who calls hope the thing with feathers.

. . .

Plus there'd been supporting plagiarisms along the way.

AARON: And, reader, you married him.

JOAN: And . . . I did.

AARON: But . . . Levittown?

JOAN: Oh, well—we had grand expectations of an ordinary life, back then.

He looks at her questioningly.

They didn't pan out.

. . .

The ring on your finger was given you by . . .

AARON: Melissa.

JOAN: Melissa!
The former Melissa . . . ?

AARON: Melissa Stanton Ames.

JOAN: This is, I take it, an exogamous marriage.

AARON: She's Episcopalian, yeah.

JOAN: Fair?

AARON: Yes.

JOAN: With air force blue eyes?

AARON: Maya blue.

JOAN: And sheaves of flaxen hair.

AARON: Ash blond and very fine.

JOAN: Fine like the hair of a balding forty-year-old man?

AARON: Like the hair of a baby.

JOAN: Do you call her "baby"?

AARON: I call her Melissa.

JOAN: In your tenderest moments?

AARON: I call her Melissa.

JOAN: Would this be lifelong policy or sad falling off?

> *Beat.*

AARON: What does Mr. Dellamond call you?

JOAN: In the privacy of his mind?
    I have no idea, I *shudder* to—
    At tender moments
    perhaps he calls . . . someone else, I've never been sure.

AARON: Ah.

JOAN: Ah.

    Beat.

    He fought in a war. Did *you* fight in a—

AARON: No.

JOAN: You must have been the right age for Korea.

AARON: Asthma.

JOAN: Is that why you're blocked?

AARON: Oh, but I'm not—

JOAN: Yes-yes-yes, but is it that?
    The absence of a good
    proving war?
    Something that certifies you forever?

AARON: You don't see me.

    Pause.

JOAN: I would like to try.

AARON: You see this person— One piece published some time ago
in a prestigious but little-read journal and you
—go all American— You think:
stoppage—failure—why aren't you *rushing* somewhere? but
. . .
Some silences are meditations.
Some silences are gatherings. Think the Duino Elegies.
Think
. . .
. . .
the Duino Elegies—
this astonishing masterpiece brooded over for an eternity
then emerging in a single breath.
. . .
I'm a patient worker. Not blocked,
not stalled
. . .
gradual.
See me like that.

JOAN: I will.

AARON: No, no, please.
See me like that because that's who I am.

Beat.

JOAN: I *will.*

Beat. Sincerely:

So, when your brooding is over, you'll produce something along the lines of the Duino Elegies?

Beat.

AARON: I'm sure the ladies have driven home by now.

JOAN: I'm sure they haven't.
They klatch for hours at a stretch.
They have so much to say and they say it so joyously. Where do you suppose they find all that glee?

AARON (SHRUGS): . . . Some people are happy.

JOAN: Don't be ridiculous.

He laughs, quite suddenly.

She looks at him, smiles.

He smiles back.

I can talk to you.

AARON: *I* can talk to *you.*

Silence. There's all kinds of radiance to it.

A moment. They move awkwardly at the same time, she toward him, he to go.

JOAN: Aaron.

He stops.

AARON: Umm . . . ?

JOAN: Mr. Port.

AARON: . . . Yes?

JOAN: I want to write something.

AARON: . . . I know.

JOAN: No—you don't understand—I *truly* want to write something.
. . .
I'm not here because French Cooking wouldn't have me or there were no seats left in Current Affairs in the World and Elsewhere; I am not here for the coffee breaks and the malice. I'm here because I *need* to write.

AARON: Then do. *Do.*

JOAN: You don't understand.

AARON: I'm trying.

JOAN: I've begun to mutter in the supermarket. Like a crazy woman—
like a crazy woman!
Mutter mutter mutter—these monologues! Screeds . . .
Scenes . . .
and epigrams while staring at a cutlet in a freezer case—but I never write them down.
I'm suffering from
. . . Acute Repressed Graphomania!

AARON: Then why *don't* you write them down?

JOAN: Because I'm afraid of what will happen on the page!

> . . .

I'm afraid of what I'll see there. Things I don't know I know.
Pages that can't be ripped up. Indelible things.

AARON: . . . But that's what you want.

JOAN: Don't be soft-minded. You know what I mean.

AARON: Then you just have to smash everything up.

> *Beat. She stares at him.*

You don't have a choice.
Listen:
The things that stop us writing are the things that *stop* us.
What are you protecting? People's feelings?
Whose? Friends?
You say you haven't got any. Your marriage?
Please.
Some notion of family or reputation or some financial—
some *job* you're holding on to? See? There's nothing.
You have to be ruthless.
You have to . . . let the chips fall. You *don't have a choice*.

JOAN: Is that how *you* are?
Would you . . . *smash* everything?

AARON: In a minute.

JOAN: You're terrifying.

> . . .

> I'm *ter*rified.

> . . .

> What do I do? What do I *do*?

> *Pause.*

> *He looks at her with sympathy.*

> *He has something to say, doesn't know if he wants to say it. Decides to.*

AARON: You don't have to tell the truth, you know.

> . . .

> You can lie.
> It's all right to lie.

JOAN (PLAINTIVELY): I don't think I know *how*.

> *Lights.*

AARON: And then, home.

> *Lights change.*

The train at night is overlit in that way that makes everyone look like a criminal and something troubles me,
something that hasn't made its way into words yet, a question I never dreamed I'd ask myself, something like:
Was I a bad teacher tonight?
I dismiss it—and sink into the lovely ritual shucking off of Levittown.
Suddenly I'm in the bleak new Penn Station

and there's the usual disappointment of homecoming: Nobody's thrown me a parade.

On the subway

I run into my close friend Jay Beckerhoff.

This is a hideous nightmare.

Jay appears.

Jay's first novel has been showing up on the standard Most Promising lists (ho hum:

Prelude to Oblivion).

But also he's recently lost sixty pounds and become handsome,

which is unforgivable. You look great, Jay.

Jay sighs heavily.

Now that he's deliriously happy, he's chronically world-weary, the phony bastard.

JAY: When I was fat, I had only one problem; now I have multitudes.

AARON: Fleetingly, I envy Jay his former avoirdupois and consider gaining weight:

How wonderful if all my problems could resolve into a sharp and easily solvable one!

This is madness.

JAY: And *you?*

What's next for *you?*

AARON: *He's* currently weltering in the quiet frenzy of a small success, so the burden, of course, is on me to answer this terrible question.

Beckerhoff is always trumping you like that. Beckerhoff claims to be friends with John Updike—

JAY: Updike's lumbago's acting up.

AARON: —though there is no record of Updike claiming to be friends with Beckerhoff. Congratulations on the novel, Jay.

It's doing nicely.

And do I detect him wincing? He should be.

The novel features an extended passage he baldly stole from me. I don't mention this because it's the same passage I baldly stole from James Joyce: Joke's on Beckerhoff.

So, Jay: Is there going to be a second novel?

I know that's the hell part—

JAY: Almost done.

AARON: Oh. What's it about?

JAY: I'm finally confronting my memories of Korea.

JAY AND AARON: The cold! The bone-crushing cold!

JAY: Of course, I'm using Korea as a metaphor for Vietnam.

AARON (TO US): Brilliant. In my new story I'm using my shoes as a metaphor for my sneakers.

JAY: But you?

Tell me, really: What's *next* for you?

Beat.

AARON (TO US): Why are we so insistent on the future?
　　Why can't we simply be *here* and now on the train?
　　But of course even the train's conveying me to the future, the
unchanging one:
　　home and its woes. I say nothing.

JAY: Okay, in that case, where ya coming *from*?

AARON: I consider lying. Instead:
　　Levittown.

　　Like a dirty joke:

　　I teach adult ed.
　　I make it sound louche;
　　my tone is dense with implication.

JAY (NEUTRAL): Oh.

AARON: Well . . . they *think* I'm there to teach.

JAY: Uh-huh.
　　What *are* you there to do?

AARON (IMPROV): Can't tell you! But I promise you:
　　No Teaching Will Transpire on My Watch.

JAY: That's sick, Aaron.
　　Are you *writing* something? Is a *woman* mixed up in this?

AARON: I give a half smile. I go mute.
　　In my silence I decide
　　I am writing something; there is a woman mixed up in this.
　　Extraordinary.

We arrive at our stop.
Beckerhoff and I part, trading ambiguities.

To Jay:

Survive this.
I know it can be monstrous.

JAY: And your situation, God!

AARON: Courage.

JAY: Keep the faith.

AARON: *Merde.*

Jay exits.

I trot to my apartment
puffed up with guilt and intrigue and sabotage and romance,
with the certain promise of a future and no idea what's
what.
The week somehow passes.
And the next week there's an absence
and I wonder if I've caused it—by saying the wrong thing,
by failing some secret test.

The next week.

All the students are there except Joan.

ANNA: Europe was the trip of a lifetime.
My husband, who is something of an amateur art histo-
rian, kept pointing out columns and telling us what kind they
were.

"That's Ionic." "That's Doric." "That's Corinthian." I tell you, it was an education being with him. The children seemed to enjoy themselves as well.

I liked all the cities, though Lucerne smelled like manure. I think my favorite was Venice. Venice is a study in contrasts. The rich, the poor. The clean, the squalid. It really teaches you something.

The whole family returned feeling very satisfied that we were able to afford such an educational and entertaining journey.

The End.

She pauses.

AARON: Comments? . . . Anyone?

Beat.

FRIEDA: Where's the hatred?

ANNA: Frieda!

FRIEDA: I know your family—I'm your next-door neighbor. So it's incumbent on me to ask: Where's the hatred?

AARON: That was a piece of travel writing.

FRIEDA: The hatred, the hatred!

AARON: I don't know, Mrs. Cohen, that that's necessary . . . given the subject . . . and style.

FRIEDA: But—

AARON: It's . . . not apropos.

FRIEDA: . . . I know the family: I missed the hatred. That's all.

>   *Awkwardness.*

AARON: . . . Anyone else?

MIDGE: I liked when you wrote that Venice was a study in contrasts.

ANNA (STILL QUIETLY SEETHING): It is.
>   It's a study in contrasts.

MIDGE: I thought the phrase was very evocative. I felt like I was there
>   with you.

ANNA: That's what I wanted.

MIDGE: "A study in contrasts"—
>   I could smell canals, no, very nice, Anna.

>   *Pause.*

JACK: Can I talk?

AARON: Mr. Hassenpflug, of course.

JACK: The story I read . . . the other week.

AARON: Yes.

JACK: I thought it was very powerful.

AARON: Good.

JACK: I thought it was a very powerful piece.

AARON: Good.

JACK: I found it very moving. I was very moved by it.
I feel others must have been, too.

AARON: . . . I can't speak for others.

JACK: I've changed some words.
Is it all right if I read it again?

AARON: . . .
. . .
We do have time?
No one else has anything to . . . ? We do have time.
. . .
Are there any objections?
. . .
. . .
Go ahead, Mr. Hassenpflug.

JACK: I fought in the Battle of Overloon. It was a big mess.
There was a lot of death and bloodshed, including my friends.
I was badly injured but kept going.
I still dream of it sometimes and I guess I wake up scream-
ing because my wife is looking at me and she says,
"That again?" The End.

He looks up, proud, with tears streaming down his face.

I think it gets better every time. Do others feel that?

Pause.

Another pause.

FRIEDA: Yes, Jack. We do.
    That silence you heard just now:
    That was us assimilating what you've given us.
    You know what that story was, Jack? Succinct.

JACK (TO AARON): Is succinct good?

FRIEDA: Succinct is excellent.
    You've moved us, Jack, bravo.

JACK: I thought because getting this out it's
    kind of changed my life a little bit and I thought
    If You Move Yourself, You Must Move Others. Is that a rule?

AARON: I don't really believe in rules.

FRIEDA: It *is* a rule, Jack. Our first rule.
    I'm writing it down.

AARON: I've been ... overruled, ha-ha.

    A vague moment.

FRIEDA: She's not coming this week, Mr. Port.

AARON: ... Pardon me?

FRIEDA: Mrs. Dellamond.
    Class is almost over; she's not gonna show.

AARON: No, of course not.

FRIEDA: That's why your eyes keep . . . isn't it?

AARON: I wasn't aware that my eyes—

FRIEDA: Yes, they are, but to no avail; she won't be joining us tonight. Perhaps you said something to scare her in your after-class tête-à-tête. I have no way of knowing.

But if we may invite you back into the room for a moment to join the *others* who've paid a fee, I'd like once again to request an assignment.

AARON: As I've said: I don't really care for—

FRIEDA: But other than that we live in the age of anything goes, you've never offered a reason for your distaste.

AARON: An assignment would be strictly an expression of my own interest. Why should what interests me interest you?

FRIEDA: Uh-huh. I see.

So you don't give assignments.

AARON: No.

FRIEDA: And you don't believe in rules.

AARON: Not really.

FRIEDA: You're not much of a teacher, are you, Mr. Port?

Sounds of protest.

Well, it's the elephant in the room.

JACK: I don't think that. I'm getting a lot out of this class.

ANNA: I don't agree at all. I think he's doing an excellent job, Frieda.
We read what we write—he says, "Any comments?"—what else is there? What, do you want he should do your writing for you?

FRIEDA: I simply didn't expect
(and there's no reason to jump down my throat, Anna)
I simply didn't expect there would be such a high degree of nothing from him—we read, he says two syllables, we talk— forgive me:
I didn't know I'd be studying with a Freudian.

MIDGE: I don't agree with Frieda, either, completely.
People teach how they teach and we should go along with it; they're the experts.
But I *also* feel it'd be helpful if we were told what to write from time to time.
Because my one piece is, frankly, the one really unusual event in my life that I'd be willing to write about.
I mean, every week I put aside time to sit down and write and I find I'm out of material—I'm blocked!

FRIEDA: And how can you help Midge with that problem, Mr. Port? If you'd be so good as to have the energy.

AARON: . . . Why do you think you have to write only about unusual events?

MIDGE: What else?

AARON: What happens in your everyday life?

MIDGE: Nothing happens in my everyday life.

AARON: Look close enough and I'm sure you'll find it's grotesque.

A hitch.

And, of course, sublime.

Beat.

I mean,
if you weren't so fuc—damned conventional
when you considered your lives, I think you'd find
they *breed* stories—
Look—you live in a small place at a certain time
among a few people—
The very con*fine*ment of it: Aren't there coincidences?
Don't they, sometimes, delight you or seem to you like
fate?
That's *form*.
Look— What makes writing a story hard? Okay: everything,
but what's *hardest*?
Finding an ending. Well, it sounds to me when you speak
about your lives, that there are nothing but endings. Endings—
everywhere!
Limitations, dead ends—aborted—*endings*!

*He makes a gesture as if it's hopeless; he's obscurely
angry.*

Beat.

ANNA: So: The World Around Us, you're saying.

AARON: Yes.

ANNA: Write about that.

AARON: Yes.

MIDGE: Do you do that?

AARON: Of course.

MIDGE: We're in the world around you. Do you write about us?

AARON: This is off-limits.

> *Beat.*

FRIEDA: But say you're desperate—

AARON: I'm not desperate—

FRIEDA: But say you *are*:
How off-limits would we be then?

ANNA: I don't want to suddenly find I'm "grotesque" in a Literary Guild selection—

MIDGE: I don't want to be turned into a mockery in the pages of *The New Yorker*—

FRIEDA: I don't think we have to worry about the pages of *The New*

Yorker—but even in some crappy *Pennysaver*-type thing people use to wrap the fish—it's in print.

Beat.

AARON: You have nothing to worry about. My solemn word.

Lights.

A week passes.

Anna is there. Frieda enters.

FRIEDA: Anna! Hello! Look what I have: A Story!
At long last and a shocker!

ANNA (CHILLY): That's good.

FRIEDA: Why did you and Abe go without me?

ANNA: What are we, the Three Musketeers, joined at the hip?

FRIEDA: It just seems a waste of gas.

ANNA: Negligible.

Beat.

FRIEDA: All right: What's up with you?

ANNA: I'm not sure I'm speaking to you right now.

FRIEDA: Not sure or not?

ANNA: I don't know.

FRIEDA: Why?
How have I transgressed?

ANNA (WITH HATRED): "The hatred." "The hatred."

FRIEDA: We're supposed to be truthful.

ANNA: I was not being untruthful.

FRIEDA: I hear the screaming next door.

ANNA: This was not about that. This was a different topic.

FRIEDA: That's a cop-out.

ANNA: . . .
It's not your place to decide. You're not the lawgiver here.

FRIEDA: Let's not be selective, Anna. It's not as if you're the soul of
discretion. Last night you took it to the lawn.

ANNA: For two seconds.
My God, you've got ears like rabbit ears—

FRIEDA: I was taking out the garbage.
You don't want to take it to the lawn. You'll become like the
Schaeffers, another Greek drama every night.

ANNA: This was a one-time thing.

I made the mistake of escaping for a minute—who knew he'd follow?

FRIEDA: What was it about?

ANNA: This class.

FRIEDA: Why shouldn't you take a class?
He's two hallways away as we speak, sculpting fat women in bikinis.

ANNA: *What* I write.

FRIEDA: You write ditties.

ANNA: He doesn't know that.

FRIEDA: He hasn't read it?

ANNA: No.

FRIEDA: Then I have a simple solution:

ANNA: No!
Can I have something of my own?
Does he have to have his nose in all my business? But this is not the point.
The point is, it's not for you to go spreading my private affairs.

FRIEDA: These people don't care.

ANNA: It could get back to others who do.

FRIEDA: What? Like who?

ANNA: The children. Okay?
The children could find out.

Beat.

FRIEDA: You're right and I apologize.

Anna's skeptical.

This is sincere.
Children are the uncrossable line.

ANNA: We keep it from them.
We only fight when they're asleep.
Why should they be party to our misery?

FRIEDA: I'm very sorry, Anna.

ANNA: I don't tell them these things.
Whatever strife may be in the marriage. Or what happened
to Miri. Or the world in general! We live in terrible times; they
don't need to know about it, they just need to feel safe.

FRIEDA: You're absolutely right. This is how I raised my kids.

ANNA: And it worked, didn't it?

FRIEDA: With Brian, beautifully. With Todd, the jury's out.

ANNA: This stinking war.

FRIEDA: I've put my feelings about it on hold.

ANNA: You've had to.

FRIEDA: I've had to.

. . .

Though he says he pushes pencils.

He says they think his intelligence makes him too valuable to do anything useful.

ANNA: He's always had a high IQ, hasn't he?

FRIEDA: One-fifty, one-sixty, they can't even measure it.

ANNA: He should have gone to college for the student deferment.

FRIDA: For the love of learning. For the *job* opportunities.

I don't know what's what with him. I've done my best.

I've shielded him.

And ours is a happy home. Lou and I, knock wood.

What bad there was they never saw.

We've lived here his whole life—since before he was born.

Brooklyn, that mishegas, the street life—

not even a distant memory for him. It's always been the lawn, the yard.

ANNA: Brian, at least—

FRIEDA: Brian is an angel. Brian never complains.

Brian lives up to his potential.

ANNA: He's quiet but you always know he's thinking. That sly smile.

FRIEDA: Brian's at peace with himself. Todd . . .
    Well, listen, he's young.

ANNA: You never know.

A moment. They think about this. Joan enters.

JOAN (STIFF SMILE): Are we the first?

FRIEDA (WITH HIGH PLEASANTNESS): Mrs. Dellamond, you're back! You've been missed.

JOAN: . . . I have to make a phone call.

She exits.

FRIEDA (STILL PLEASANT, CALLING AFTER HER): The pay phone is broken!

They listen to the sound of her retreating footsteps.

I don't care for her.

ANNA: Why not?

FRIEDA: Who is she and what's she been doing here all these years if she hasn't been doing anything?

ANNA: She seems perfectly nice.

62

FRIEDA: No.

> She doesn't.

> At best she seems *im*perfectly nice and I'm just acknowledging the possi*bil*ity. Why is she so critical?

ANNA: She hardly ever *says* anything.

FRIEDA: And her silence is pure criticism.

ANNA: How do you figure?

FRIEDA: You know why I don't like the silent? Because you cannot win an argument with someone who isn't arguing.

> It can't be done!

> I don't think that's fair. It's not democratic!

> There they stand,

> with their superior little quietness: the winner by virtue of having forfeited the match—

> what is that? She's *scornful*, this Joan,

> with her hair and cheekbones and mockery.

ANNA: Sometimes people are offended by people who just turn out to be shy.

> *Midge enters.*

MIDGE: What'd I miss?

ANNA: Frieda's not so crazy about this Joan.

MIDGE: Oh, Frieda never likes pretty girls.

FRIEDA: What?

MIDGE: It's true.

FRIEDA: You're spouting nonsense.

ANNA: She has a theory.

MIDGE: Tell me the theory.

ANNA: She's so quiet that she's critical.

FRIEDA: That's not it!

MIDGE: Frieda never likes the pretty girls.

FRIEDA: Ugh! I'm done with you both.

> *Jack enters, followed by Marc.*

> Jack!

JACK: Hi.

FRIEDA: I just want you to know: I'm still thinking about your story.

JACK: Really?

FRIEDA: I woke up thinking about it this very morning.

JACK: No kidding.

FRIEDA: It's so strong that you really don't have to read it to us ever
again.

JACK: No?

FRIEDA: In fact, it would be a mis*take* to. It would diminish it.

Aaron enters.

AARON: Good evening.

FRIEDA: Mr. Port! Mr. Port!

AARON: Yes, Mrs. Cohen?

FRIEDA: I found some shame!

AARON: . . .
Good.

FRIEDA: I rummaged through the distant past and remembered a moment.
I have the story.

AARON: Then you'll be reading for us?

FRIEDA: I'll be reading.

AARON: We can all breathe a sigh of relief.

Joan enters.

Mrs. Dellamond.

JOAN: Hi.

AARON: How *good*—you're *back*.

JOAN: Yes.

AARON: I— You've been missed.

JOAN: I was working. I was *writing*.

AARON: You— *Really?*

JOAN: What you said—
>   I decided I wouldn't come back until I *had* something—

AARON: Do you—
>   Have you *brought* something?

JOAN: I have.

AARON: Well! Wonderful!

>   *Beat.*

>   So we have *two* people reading today—what a bounty. So.
>   Let's start. Um.
>   Which of you would . . . Mrs. Cohen?

FRIEDA: I'll let Mrs. Dellamond go first.

JOAN: Oh, you can—

FRIEDA: I'd prefer to go second.
>   What I've written is a cornucopia of shame and it will re-
>   quire a lengthy response.

AARON: All right, then. Mrs. . . .

Joan takes stage.

Lights shift.

JOAN: It was her first week in the town. There had been no greeting, no band, no cake, no covered dish. They were not the original owners of this house but they came full of hope, or at least her husband did.

These were the days when she was trying to get pregnant, though God knew what they'd do for money. But she strenuously tracked when she ovulated, for they were on a sex budget.

This was to be one of their evenings.

It was a warm day and she sat in the living room chair. The door was open because of the heat, but, more, because she was hoping to be welcomed.

Of course it's possible she fell asleep. It might have been a dream.

Not knowing would torment her for decades: In any event, this is what she believed took place. She closed her eyes and when she opened them again, a baby was disporting itself in her living room.

This can all be a mime thing:

A baby crawls into her living room. It feels right at home.

There's some soft, perhaps nervous laughter from the class.

MIDGE (SOFTLY TO ANNA): Remember, that sometimes happened with the toddlers?

ANNA: All the houses looked the same to them.

Jack shushes them.

JOAN: There was something confident about this trespassing infant and she was terrified of it—terrified as if it had been a mouse or a roach or any weak, harmless thing that scares us simply because it's out of place.

She might have stepped outside and called to her neighbors—she knew they were out there; she'd been hearing a fracas of them for some time.

But she had not yet met or even seen these people and she was so afraid of being shunned. The infant was not to be deflected. Clearly a baby with imperialist tendencies, it continued to reconnoiter what she still only so tentatively thought of as "her" living room.

Then, without warning, it stopped.

It stopped as though it had fallen asleep, but it was not asleep. It was content.

It had chosen her.

For an infinite moment, they stared at each other; it was a standoff. At last, she did the only thing she could.

*Joan kicks the baby out, a steady series of kicks. Anna
and Midge whoop. Jack chuckles.*

Luckily, this baby, seemingly so adventuresome, was, in truth, the spirit of inertia incarnate—it would tend to rest or move as it was acted upon. A little boot over the threshold and it was gone, before she even learned its sex. She closed the door, locked it, and returned to her chair. She was alone, true enough, but she was uncaught.

The End.

Beat.

AARON (BEAMING): Well!
. . .
Comments?

FRIEDA: What *was* that?

AARON: Mrs. Cohen—

FRIEDA: Who *is* this person—

MIDGE: What's the problem, Frieda?

ANNA (OVERLAPS): I thought it was imaginative.

AARON: I'd appreciate it if you would confine your comments to—

FRIEDA: Was that a provocation of some kind? Was that an *insult*?

JOAN: I—

MIDGE: Sit down, Frieda.

ANNA (SIMULTANEOUSLY): It was a *story*.

FRIEDA: I'm sorry, I can't stay!
I just remembered a previous engagement!

AARON: Mrs.—

FRIEDA: I have to be elsewhere.

She leaves.

A moment.

JOAN: I just told the truth.
I decided to tell the truth.
Wasn't that supposed to be the better choice?

End Act One.

Act Two

Frieda sits, alone in the room.

Joan enters.

FRIEDA: Oh, hello.

JOAN: . . . Hello?

FRIEDA: Just us.

JOAN: Is it just us?

FRIEDA: So far.

    Pause.

    The snow.

JOAN: Driving was a bear.

FRIEDA: I walked.

JOAN: *Did* you?

FRIEDA: I walked from my home.

JOAN: . . . Is that far?

FRIEDA: Peasant stock.

JOAN: Oh.

FRIEDA: It toughens you.
> Putsches, pogroms, long walks; my ancestry.
>
> *Beat.*

JOAN: Does the pay phone in the hall—?

FRIEDA: No, it doesn't.
> *Beat.*

JOAN: I think they might have fixed—

FRIEDA: It's just us,
> till the others arrive, which they may not. Even Mr. Port—

JOAN: He hasn't.

FRIEDA: No-o-o, he has not.
> *Joan sits, fusses with her folder.*

> Have you written yet another epic to delight us with?

JOAN: . . . Not an epic.

FRIEDA: Ah

. . .

. . .

. . .

So tell me a little about yourself.

JOAN: . . . Why?

FRIEDA: Because we're here and talking is all there is. There's nothing else. For instance: How many children do you have?

JOAN: I don't have any children.

FRIEDA: I thought not.

> *Joan looks at her questioningly.*

Your story last week.

JOAN: Oh . . . that was just a story.

FRIEDA: Of course. Oh, of course!

Still, you share with your heroine the trait of childlessness?

JOAN: I have no children.

FRIEDA: I gleaned that.

. . .

. . .

Then why do you live here?

JOAN: I'm sorry?

FRIEDA: It's a simple question.
What does Levittown offer you?
And what do you offer in return?

Pause.

JOAN: Tell me about your children.

FRIEDA: Oh, there's so much to tell. I wouldn't know where to start.

JOAN: How many do you have?

FRIEDA: Two boys.

JOAN: What ages?

FRIEDA: Todd is nineteen and Brian is seventeen.

JOAN: What are they like?

FRIEDA: Brian, that's my youngest, is studious. Brian doesn't say much.
Brian has a sly smile—he knows things. Todd is in Vietnam.

JOAN: That's awful.

FRIEDA: I beg your pardon?

JOAN: I'm appalled by the war.

FRIEDA: That's very fashionable.

JOAN: I'm sincere.

FRIEDA: Also fashionable.

JOAN: Couldn't he get into college?

FRIEDA: . . .
    Answering you would imply I consider the question remotely acceptable.

JOAN: I'm sorry.
    I just can't imagine—

FRIEDA: He was offered a full scholarship to Hofstra, though there was no financial need.
    He was offered a partial to Adelphi. The state schools clamored.
    He went
    for reasons that remain his own.
    . . .

JOAN: I see.

FRIEDA: The childless . . .
    . . .

She lets the phrase dangle because she thinks it speaks for itself.

But you—*you.*
I can't picture your life. I can't picture your day. I try.
What was it Mr. Port called that? Sympathetic Imagination?
I try to sympathetically imagine you. I find I can't.

Beat.

What use do you make of this place if there's never been a
baby?

You don't

attend PTA meetings, or Little League games. You don't car-
pool,

you don't even buy in bulk.

. . .

I'm not suggesting

that these are the

Cultural Advantages of Levittown. *But*

they are the points of entry. You say,

Toddy had such a bad reaction to the Sabin vaccine. Midge
says, For Stewie it was nothing.

All of a sudden, a topic has developed. The mystery of how
children differ. What a funny thing, one of you says. Such a
funny thing, says the other.

Did he drink milk before taking it? you ask. Yes, the other says.

A little light science ensues:

Ruthie's Ava also drank milk before and was fine. It's the
milk that makes the vaccine tolerable.

You share a tiny triumph. You've figured something out.

You're a slightly grander person than you were that morning. This is motherhood.

Neighborliness.

Purpose and Competence. This is meaning.

And for me it's wonderful. It's a wonderment.

. . .

. . .

JOAN: Why do you dislike me, Mrs. Cohen?

FRIEDA: Where did *that* come from?

JOAN: Have I offended you?

FRIEDA: I don't know what you're talking about. I don't dislike you.
I barely *know* you.

JOAN: Last week you stormed out—

FRIEDA: I remembered an obligation—

JOAN: There's a hostility that comes off you—

FRIEDA (OVERLAPS): No no no no no—
Sometimes people from your part of the world (where is it
you come from again?) . . .

JOAN: My father was military; we—

FRIEDA: Sometimes people who come from nowhere
· mistake my breezy truthful manner for brusqueness. Of
course I don't dislike you.
Of course I don't.
. . .
. . .
. . .
Who could dislike a person who kicks babies?

JOAN: One baby!

FRIEDA: Oh! A dilettante—I stand corrected—

JOAN: That was fiction.

FRIEDA: I know a roman à clef when I see one and *that* was a roman à—

JOAN: Just because you utterly lack imagination—

FRIEDA: I don't require an imagination!

    I have always found the facts before my face interesting enough, thank you very much, and the latest fact is: You're a baby kicker.

JOAN: It is dismaying that . . .

    not only do you lack imagination yourself,

    you cannot conceive that it might exist in others.

    . . .

    . . . That is in*or*dinately sad.

    . . .

    It would be tragic if . . . well.

    Aaron enters.

AARON: Sorry I'm so late.

    The trains were a disaster.

    . . .

    Is it just us three?

FRIEDA: As of yet.

AARON: Ah.

    A moment. Tense.

Marc enters, snow crusted.

MARC: Hello . . . hello . . .

> *He takes his seat.*

AARON: Well.
> Given the time . . . and the weather,
> I don't anticipate the others showing up so . . .
> Do any of you
> . . . ?

> *No response.*

> Mrs. Cohen, have you reconsidered reading your piece from last week?

FRIEDA: I won't be reading my piece from last week and haven't yet embarked on another.

> *Silence.*

AARON: All right.
> Mr. Adams . . . ?

MARC: I'm working very hard.

> *Beat.*

AARON: Okay.
> Mrs.—

JOAN: I've brought something.

AARON: You have?

JOAN: I've been writing a lot, I've been writing very hard, most of it's miscellany, random, I don't know what you call it, I throw it in a shoe box, but this is a sort of play, a very *brief*—

AARON: Please . . .

Jack, Anna, and Midge enter in a flurry.

ANNA: You didn't wait, Frieda.

FRIEDA: I thought you weren't coming.

JACK (SIMULTANEOUSLY WITH ABOVE): What a blizzard, huh! Not a fit night for man or—oh oh oh, she's gonna read!

They settle.

JOAN: It's just a fragment.

AARON: That's enough.

She stands. Lights.

JOAN: One afternoon her husband came to her and said:

HUSBAND (ENTERS): I didn't go to the city today.

JOAN: Were you not feeling well?

HUSBAND: I felt fine.

JOAN: Were you fired?

HUSBAND: No.

JOAN: Then what?

HUSBAND: I don't work there anymore.

JOAN: Do you work?

HUSBAND: Yes.

JOAN: Where do you work?

HUSBAND: Here.
   In town. At TSS.

   She stares at him.

   In the hardware department. I know you don't shop there so I thought I'd be pretty safe and you have no friends
   and I have so few.
   I figured if I ever ran into one of them, I could ditch my store coat and pretend to be a shopper.
   It was a risky proposition.
   Finally, the tension became unbearable. That's why I'm telling you now.
   The city gave me vertigo.
   It made me faint like a woman. I can't go there anymore.

JOAN: Then . . . this is where we conduct our lives? This is the whole
   of it?

HUSBAND: Yes.

> *Beat.*

> *She punches him.*

> *Lights.*

> *A moment.*

> *Another moment.*

AARON: . . . Comments?

FRIEDA: Mr. Port, a question?

AARON: Yes.

FRIEDA: If I recall correctly,
> Mrs. Dellamond's last story concluded with the kicking of a baby.
> And the denouement of this one
> involves the punching of a husband. Tell me:
> Would you say this constitutes a genre?

AARON: No.
> Any other—

FRIEDA: A tendency?

AARON: No.
> Anyone else—

FRIEDA: Could you answer me a question, then?

AARON: I . . . suppose so.

FRIEDA: Why does it seem that the literature the critics like
    is the kind with violence and conflict?

AARON: I don't know that that's true.

FRIEDA: It's true.

AARON: I'm not certain that's true.

FRIEDA: It's *true*.

AARON: Well,
    if it is true
    I suppose it's because
    they're what makes long forms possible.
    Take these qualities away and you have at most
    a lyric poem,
    which can be lovely
    but is outside the mesh of narrative.

FRIEDA: *Why?*
    Why do you *say* that?

AARON: I think I explained—

FRIEDA: Listen:
    In the summer
    I can smell the neighbors barbecuing: Tears come to my eyes.
    In fall, there's the burning of leaves: It's a concerto for the nose.
    Why can't this be a story?

AARON: I suppose
     after a few sentences you'd find it lacks drive.

FRIEDA: Drive?

AARON: The pulse,
     the *throttle*
     of history.

FRIEDA: History! History!
     What is this fixation on history?

AARON: Well—

FRIEDA: No, no, you with the asthma and the 4-F exemption, *you're*
     not explaining history to me—
     I'm gonna talk for a change.

MIDGE: Don't excite yourself, Frieda—

FRIEDA: I'm ten years old—
     A crazy ninety-year-old woman
     tries to throw herself down the stairs on a daily basis—I'm
     scooping her up—this skeleton—"Oh, Bones-and-Moans is at
     it again," my mother says—
     this is the Lower East Side and I'm not talking about the
     smelly kids saying, "Want a flower?"
     My father's a receiving clerk at this business—they resell
     dented canned goods, he dies mysteriously at fifty. My mother
     develops psychosomatic emphysema, gasps her last at fifty-eight
     listening to Pegeen Fitzgerald on the radio.

So one day I wake up in a town
that sometimes seems to be universally maligned
but I get an unobstructed view of the sunset
and you tell me this can't be a story because there's no history in it?
Let me tell you something, Mr. Port.
You'll find that in heaven (should you get there) very little happens.

AARON: Grandstands can have a certain energy, Mrs. Cohen, but I
don't appreciate attacks on members of the class
even if they are oblique and disguised.

FRIEDA: Are you suggesting that I—

AARON: I am. Yes, I am.
. . .
. . . We should be happy when we're in the company of gifted
people. We should
. . .
be happy about that.
. . .
. . .

FRIEDA: Yes.
Yes, you're right. Forgive me.
I will try to be happy when my classmates excel.
. . .
Just as *you're* ecstatic when a writer of
your own generation publishes a novel to great acclaim.

Silence.

AARON: I don't suppose anyone has brought anything else in.

Silence.

The snow is starting again.
I think, yes, I think
given the inclement conditions
there's no need to extend our evening unnaturally, so why don't we adjourn for now?

Pause.

Silence. The class, chastened, starts to go.

JACK: Your stories.

JOAN: Yes?

JACK: They're upsetting.

JOAN: . . . Okay.

JACK: I like them.

JOAN: Thank you.

JACK: I like upsetting things. They're believable.

FRIEDA: Puh!

MIDGE: I agree. They're very brave. I admire them. They're gritty. They're challenging.

FRIEDA: "Gritty."

MIDGE: So it's not your bag, Frieda—that doesn't mean it isn't good.

Just last week, Saul and I saw this play in the Village—the most meshuggener thing you ever saw

—it was in a basement!—but go know; we enjoyed it. Things are changing.

ANNA: They are; they're changing.

Jack and the women leave.

FRIEDA (PARTING SHOT): All I can say is:

How apropos that the Winds of Change come to us courtesy of a woman who for seven years never set foot out of her house.

Joan looks at her.

I *know* people.

Exits.

MARC: This was a short class.

He exits.

Just Joan and Aaron.

Silence.

JOAN: Did you read the Colette?

AARON: . . . I tried.

JOAN: You *failed*?

AARON: I couldn't see the point of it. It was . . . atmospheric?
It was just so *female* somehow. Maybe it was the translation.

She nods.

Seven years?

JOAN (SHRUGS): I'm excessive.

AARON: . . . What did you do?

JOAN: I read.
I Improved My Vocabulary Day to Day.

AARON: And then . . . emerged?

JOAN (GLIB, DEFLECTIVE): I wanted something to describe.

Beat.

AARON: You punched your husband?

JOAN: That was fic—yes.

AARON: For the same phobia that you yourself—

JOAN: Yes.

AARON: Is that fair?

JOAN (NO APOLOGY): I'm not fair.
Anyway, he's a man. He shouldn't be afraid; it's disgraceful.

Beat.

But did you *like* my story?
Do you think it's *good*?

AARON: . . . I do.

JOAN: That's all that matters.

AARON (SEMICORRECTIVE): It's promising, I mean; both your stories
have—

JOAN: I'll take that; that's enough for now.

AARON: Good.

JOAN (CONTINUOUS): In a few years I imagine it will start to sound like
a crucifixion,

AARON: Yes.

JOAN (CONTINUOUS): but for now I'll take it *gratefully*.
Tell me what's promising about it.

AARON: Oh—look—it's a very short piece, there's not that much to—

JOAN (OVERLAPS): The poems of William Carlos Williams are often
very—

AARON: It's surprising; both your pieces.

JOAN: Are they?

AARON: From *you*, yes.

When you came to me, came *here*
you were . . .
you *seemed* so afraid . . .

JOAN: I am so afraid . . .

AARON: Not in what you write . . .

JOAN: Yes! Yes! I'm afraid of all things equally—it's freeing.

AARON: Is it?

JOAN: If you let it be.
I'm your best student, Mr. Port—I've done what you told me to.
. . .
I will do what you tell me.
. . .

Hands to her face:

Oh my! I'm all riled up!

Pause. Glance out the window.

This is a mammoth storm.
You'll never make it home; I'm sure they'll shut down the trains.

AARON: They might.

Pause.

JOAN: There's a hotel that wouldn't cost you too much. Well: A Motor Lodge.

On the border of East Meadow and Uniondale, I think. Is that a border?

Oh yes you don't live here. *Any*way . . .

I'm sure they'd have a room and you could get a decent rate. If there's no train.

Or if you miss it.

. . .

You could call your wife. She would understand.

Wives do.

. . .

I would drive you there.

Beat.

AARON: There are cabs.

JOAN: Or I could drive you.

AARON: I wouldn't put you to the trouble.

JOAN: The Gateway?

AARON: Pardon?

JOAN: I think that might be the name of the motel: the Gateway.
To the world of next things, perhaps.
. . . Is that overwrought? I think I tend to the over—

AARON: Probably the trains are running.

JOAN: So what?
So what? So what?

AARON: . . . I haven't written yet today, I have to write.

JOAN: "For I have promises to break
> And miles to go before I wake."

> *Pause.*

> Oh God, another pause!
> Sometimes, you know, I think if your silences could be turned to words and your words to silence, it would be *so much nicer*!

> *A hesitation.*

AARON: Listen—I think your story was—

JOAN: Don't deflect me—

AARON: This is what you asked me for—

JOAN: This is *not* what I'm ask— Oh God—are you a nice Jewish boy?

AARON: No—

JOAN: You aren't a fag, are you?

AARON: God no—

JOAN: Have I missed something? Have I misunderstood?

AARON: You haven't.

JOAN: Then what is the *delay*?

Because—look—we may not get another blizzard.

Life

is not opportune that way. It has a tendency to stop, you know,

this terrible tendency to stop and—

AARON: Yes, but

things don't happen

just because there's a blizzard, they . . . don't.

. . .

This isn't the night.

JOAN: . . .

You're not running the clock out on me, are you?

AARON: . . . I have to get home.

. . .

*He looks around for something to gather: briefcase,
book.*

. . .

If I don't write something tonight, then I won't tomorrow;

some sort of thread will be broken and my life hangs from that thread and I want it to break,

but if it does . . .

. . .

You're—my God—astonishing, you know.

JOAN: Are you writing about me?

AARON: No.

JOAN: You should be. You should be.

She gathers her things.

What a pity—what a shame.

Lights.

AARON: The ride home is rough and endless, and in the middle of the
night
    I sit naked at the dining room table and furiously write.
    It seems to me
    this is the immemorial posture—naked and furious
    at a bare wooden table after midnight.
    I don't write about her; how can I?
    She hasn't happened yet, she's too unstill.
    At first I scribble about nothing—
    it's impossible to find a first-class subject when you haven't
had a war.
    But then I settle.
    My subject will be the others,
    these people I've been studying and storing and planning to
betray.
    They pour from me and as they do
    I'm no longer this pathetic night-tripper to Levittown. I'm a
spy—a plant—
    ruthless and hurtful—
    I try to remember them as I first saw them
    when my vision was pure—
    I edit out subsequent impressions, contradictory data.
    I capture their voices, bodies

the ignorance pretension and bigotry
and I find them turning into zoo creatures! They're rhinoc-
eroses
—no, mastodons! feeding and lowing,
too blind to know they're extinct.
It's all very funny at three in the morning, so funny
I laugh my ass off,
carrying on like some sort of malevolent Aesop
inscribing fables of Levittown. Each ends with the same
moral: In a godless universe, there can be no moral.
Near dawn,
exhausted and sublime, I fall into bed.
My wife, pliant girl, is sleeping in the spoon position.
I fit myself to it,
to the body of Melissa Port,
who lately I've been thinking of as "Any Port in a Storm." I
wake at ten.
I've slept four hours
but I can't wait I can't wait I need to seize those pages, pore
over them,
marvel
and anticipate.
Coffee clears my head and I read.
. . .

. . .
It's all wrong.
They weren't mastodons when I met them,
they weren't jokes—
What a childish thing
to transform them this way.

And what if by some fluke
this were published?
The mastodons would surely read it and the pain would last
forever.
Why? To what end?
After all
they're just people trying their best.
What's the point
of being ruthless and hurtful?
I shred the pages
and sink into my unchanged life. I must be kind,
I tell myself
I must be kind.
I'm sure this isn't good advice.
And the students suddenly erupt in prose.

Lights.

MIDGE: Forgive me if I'm whispering. Even fifteen years later
I'm afraid to say this aloud:
Once upon a time, we had some notions about social justice
and bought a few books so that we could develop them.
All at once there's a committee in Congress; it seems we're
storing contraband. My husband says:

HUSBAND: Maybe we can make them gifts.

MIDGE: I don't see it.

HUSBAND: Sacred things are to be handed down, not destroyed.

MIDGE: I think you're speaking words from another year.

HUSBAND: But—

MIDGE: You're civil service—you can't afford to be noble.

    . . . The weather cools. We decide to have a cookout. All the
    neighbors will come.

ANNA: I love October.

MIDGE: It is a cookout and a bonfire both. We feed the fire with paper.

    Newspaper and other paper shuffled into the newspaper.

    There are hamburgers and franks and tubs of salad and little
    children and babies.

    The little children think: These will be my memories. An
    adult woman,

    I don't remember who but she had a wen,

    has been charged with stoking the fire. She comes up to me
    and says:

WOMAN: "Religion is the opium of the people"?!

MIDGE: What?

WOMAN: I've been reading the kindling.

MIDGE: . . .

    Oh.

WOMAN: "Religion is the opium of the people"? Is *this* what you've
    been reading?

    A standoff.

MIDGE: I—

WOMAN: Isn't opium a drug? A narcotic?

MIDGE: Yes.

WOMAN: Are you *interested* in narcotics?

MIDGE: No.

WOMAN: I ask because—
    this is secret, I only know about it from the other lunch la-
    dies, they found marijuana on the high school premises.
    No one knows where it came from.

MIDGE: Oh.

WOMAN: They found it in the custodian's room.
    They asked Mr. Thompson, the head custodian, he denied
    any knowledge
    (he's a Negro)
    so they fired him.

MIDGE: I see.

WOMAN: I'm very concerned
    because once it's in the schools that kind of thing can mush-
    room.

MIDGE: Yes, yes.

WOMAN: So what's the interest in reading about narcotics?

MIDGE: I'm not even sure what that was that you read. Sometimes I
    buy things at library sales because they're a *penny*.

WOMAN: I see.
>Because I have children. I have children to protect.

MIDGE: Next week, the high school principal calls.

PRINCIPAL: I hear our former custodian, Roscoe Thompson, painted
>your house.

MIDGE: Oh?
>Yes, I guess he did.

PRINCIPAL: We had to let him go, you know. We found narcotics.
>He denied everything
>but you can't be too careful.

MIDGE: No.

PRINCIPAL: Sometimes people give people narcotics.
>Sometimes people take narcotics from people.

MIDGE: Is that the commutative property? Ha-ha-ha.

PRINCIPAL: All I'm advising is:
>There are other house painters you can hire.

MIDGE: My house was just recently painted; I won't need . . .

PRINCIPAL: All to the good, all to the good.

MIDGE: The End.

MARC: My mother was a lunch lady. She has a wen.

AARON: And more.

Jack reads.

JACK: This was we'd just moved in. Some guy I'd met at the VFW
   said, "Come on over"—
   he lived the other part of town—
   I still had a hitch in my step so was trying to be social so as
not to permanently give in to my gimpiness, and Theresa had
cards that night.
   The house was the same as anybody's but it was like it had
broke out in rooms—
   it was so big with people that I didn't know. The guy said:

GUY: Glad you could make it, Jack.

JACK: And there was something in his tone of voice made me think
   that this was one of those places I'd heard rumors about.

GUY: Here, drink this.

JACK: He slipped me a drink and there must have been something in
   it (yeah, right, like liquor)
      because the room got very swervy and the people seemed to
multiply.

GUY: Come with me, I think I have a present for you.

JACK: Then I was in a place that seemed strangely private for such a
   small house,
      maybe it was the bathroom—

—and there was a woman there I didn't know yet who I'll call Mimi X.

Her top was off.

MIMI X: Hello.

JACK: And even though her chest was hanging out she seemed sad to me.

Or maybe it was the liquor.

Or maybe she was just a sad person.

I mean, it was very hard to come to a decision! All I could say was,

"Theresa's playing cards,"

but I didn't know if I meant that to be

a permission or a cease-and-desist order.

MIMI X: Hello.

JACK: Whichever, it was becoming clear to me

that Mimi X and I were supposed to do something together.

Well, with the hitch in my step

and certain other physical problems I continued to

have, my body hadn't yet fully returned to my possession and it occurred to me that having sex with Mimi X

was maybe just the next thing that was going to happen to it.

So I did.

I don't remember anything about this part

except bing bang boom I was home and Theresa had had a bad time at cards.

THERESA: My fudge was not popular.

Apparently the recipe was written wrong on the box top and do you know

those *meanies discussed it?*

Like I wasn't there?

"She must have used too little sugar." "Did she put salt in this?"

Like I was an outcast. Like I wasn't in the group.

Welcome to the neighborhood.

They're not nice ladies, these Jewish ladies.

. . .

How was your party?

JACK: Fine.

. . .

That night, I dreamt of Judy Garland.

I was naked and had only one leg and she kept saying, "Right here where we live! Right here in Saint Louis!" Funny thing about that is,

I was never all that crazy about Judy Garland, though I had a buddy in the army who couldn't stop talking about her.

I said, "Yeah, she's a cute girl, but I'm a Carole Landis man myself."

And then someone told me she was under five feet tall, Garland, and I said to my buddy: "What do you do with such a short drink of water? You're finished before you even get started."

And he looked at me funny, like if I was a real man, I wouldn't be concerned about foreplay.

So anyway, I have this dream where I'm naked and an amputee and I wake up screaming and my wife says: "That again?" because she thinks it's the Battle of Overloon and I say yeah.

Then what happens is: Years go by

and Jack Jr. comes home

and he's all excited 'cause his friend's mother just asphyxiated herself in the garage.

And it's Mimi X,

who now we know a little

and everybody knows she's been catting around with John Y,

who's a big jerk and now he's even got a pompadour but Mimi X somehow considered him reason enough to kill herself.

Or maybe he's the last straw.

I think about how sad she was that first night and I'm wondering if I started her off on this road or if she was always this way

and that night I have the Garland dream again and I wake up screaming

and Terry's staring down at me and she says:

"Do you ever wish you died in the Battle of Overloon?" and I say, "Not really."

The End.

AARON: And finally . . .

JOAN: One day

or over the course of several it struck her

that her home was not her home.

She thought of it as an interior; the place where children had not been born.

It seemed at first curious then terrifying

that this was the case.

She thought: What will happen

if I wander among these few rooms exclusively for a short time?

Will they endear themselves to me? Will they become the walls of a fortress, manly with protectiveness,

or at least familiar?

Will something about them at last *correspond* to me?
And as she had no appointments
she was free to conduct her experiment. So she stayed inside.
And gradually
the house became her intimate
the way sometimes an enemy will become far closer than a friend ever can.

Seven years later, she went out again.

She expected the outdoors would be sea bright with color, the trees fruited with her unused potential.

But the day was gray, the trees were bare, and nothing happened.

So she got in her car driving badly from memory and went to the market.

When she got there, it seemed the same as it had seven years earlier. Nothing happened there either
or in the playground, or in the library.

Apparently, she was neither cause nor effect. She went home and returned to bed.

The next day she drove to May's department store. It, too, was as she'd remembered it;
under the lights, everybody's skin was the color of meat fat.

As she browsed through a revolving rack of gingham smocks, she felt a hand on her shoulder.

WOMAN: Are you Mrs. Jaynes?

JOAN: Yes.

WOMAN: How's your blood?

JOAN: Fine, fine, thank you.

WOMAN: You don't know me, do you?

I'm Sydelle Bostwick, your next-door neighbor.

JOAN: Mrs. Jaynes nodded curtly and moved on.

As she left the store, a woman handing out circulars stopped her.

NEXT WOMAN: It is you, isn't it? Sydelle told me.

JOAN: Are you my neighbor, too?

NEXT WOMAN: Rhonda Hagenbruch!

But you're not curving; why aren't you curving?

JOAN: Pardon?

NEXT WOMAN: I heard you were shaped like a dough hook.

JOAN: Who told you that?

NEXT WOMAN: Your mister.

He said you were deathly ill with diseased blood and you were confined to your bed and shaped like a dough hook.

Did you suddenly straighten up?

JOAN: Yes.

When she arrived home her husband was waiting.

HUSBAND: You went outside.

JOAN: You told the neighbors my blood was sick and I was shaped like a dough hook; you made me a grotesque.

HUSBAND: They started looking at me like I'd murdered you. I had to tell them something.

JOAN: Why not the truth?

HUSBAND: I had to tell them something *plausible*. Is everything fine now? Can we go out to eat?

JOAN: She said nothing to him; he was inessential.
     She retreated to her bedroom and locked the door.
     She was at a loss to explain this last portion of her life. Why had she immured herself?
     Why had she emerged? There were words that when you uttered them were deeds.
     "I now pronounce you man and wife," the minister says
     and all at once laws apply and events flow forth.
     Over seven years
     she had become thin as a sentence, shadowy as a prayer.
     She wanted more.
     She continued to stumble into the everyday world and one day on a whim
     she enrolled in a class.
     There was a man there
     who was handsome and had about him a pleasant promise of violence.
     . . .
     And they could converse!
     . . .
     With her habit of contraction,
     she decided he was the whole world, her every hope.
     But though he talked a big game, he did little,
     and made pitiful excuses not to act.

Time and opportunity passed
and she started to feel the old desperation return, that force
that had interrupted her.
She scrounged pandered trawled surveilled
for something to rescue her
for the word that would be a deed.
At last one night
surrounded by witnesses, she stood up
and said to him:
"Will you just, for God's sake, put aside your misgivings and
fuck me?"

She stands.

Turns to Aaron.

Then this happened:

Lights as she returns to her seat.

The class is frozen.

Silence.

Then:

FRIEDA: Comments?

Lights.

AARON: The final class.

The students gathered.

AARON: Well. Well.
We're all here. Surprising.
We've made it through the entire term. Isn't that something?

I see there are cupcakes; someone brought . . . cupcakes. Feel free.

We've had quite a haul, rockier than expected. No need for a *summa,*

or to waste any more time.

I don't suppose anyone has brought anything to read for our last class?

Marc's hand shoots up.

Mr., um, Adams? Really?
Would this be from your magnum opus? Well, then.
Please.

MARC: This is from my magnum opus.

Reads:

The typical New Englander of the era was more sawyer than axman, more given to the building up than the tearing down. We overstate his Puritanism.

His daily life was devoted to civic affairs, to the creation of a township, a community. The stocks were by no means the center of his life.

They were more like our stop signs—intended to regulate human traffic, to stave off chaos in a formative and unstable time.

As to his vaunted prudishness about sex, families often boasted ten, even twelve children, evidence enough that his appetites were as strong and indulged as our own, though usually within the strictures of the law.

I believe it is important that we re-see this community so that it will enable us to re-see our own: its philosophies, ordinances, achievements, disappointments, high ideals, and human digressions.

He sits down.

AARON: And then good-bye.

Class readies to leave.

JACK (TO AARON): I—
This has been a very
eye-opening experience for me.
If my wife lets me, I
may take it again next year.

AARON: He doesn't.
He tries woodworking, drops out early,
has a life,
is lost track of.

Jack nods, exits.

MARC: Good-bye . . . good-bye.

AARON: Good-bye, Mr., um, Adams.
He goes
and continues working on his magnum opus for thirty-nine years
during which he lives with his mother in their tiny house, the original model. The pages pile,
they bulge out the windows; it's noticed.
In the nineties, when outsider art becomes popular, an anthropologist drops by.
Excerpts are published, debated.
Passages of genius alternate with gibberish.
A small cult of personality develops around him; dissipates.

In 2007, there's a fire, perhaps accidental; he, his ninety-two-year-old mother,

and the magnum opus are incinerated.

Marc exits.

ANNA: Thank you, Mr. Port.

I found this very stimulating.

Tell me: What *do* you think of Gore Vidal?

AARON: She returns next year

to write about her bitter mother and Richard Nixon, separately.

Her husband, Abe, joins her in the class. Running out of material,

she revises the story of her trip to Europe. The following week, Abe writes:

ABE: In August, the couple and their fat twins took a two-week package tour to see the important cities of Europe plus Innsbruck. Upon their return, the wife telephoned everyone she knew and told them that Venice was a study in contrasts.

"Marsha? Hi. Venice is a study in contrasts." "Rita? Hi. Venice is a study in contrasts." "Corrinne? Hi. Venice is a study in contrasts." "Lucille? Hi. Venice is a study in contrasts."

The End.

He looks up. There is a silence. He leaves.

AARON: They drop the class.

A few months later, they move to a larger house in Merrick and continue their terrible marriage.

Her son will become a promising violist. When he's a young teenager, she'll escort him to the city Saturday mornings so that he can take lessons at Juilliard.

One day while waiting for him on a park bench, she'll meet a man of dubious value;

they'll have a brief affair.

She won't speak of it for thirty years. Then she will.

Anna exits.

Mrs. Braverman, good-bye.

MIDGE: Thank you—I enjoyed the course,

the craziest things happened, didn't they?

AARON: She outgrows adult ed and finds other pursuits. In 1974 she spends a week at an ashram and when she returns gazes lovingly at her friends and relatives in a manner they find disconcerting. She screams primally, eats papaya, listens to Jacques Brel, is happy.

Her sons, Stewart and Michael, attend the same midwestern university, where, having inherited their parents' interest in social justice, they protest the war. In the early seventies, they join a cult of Far Left extremists led by a charismatic man with a Jewish name. By the mid-eighties the press is routinely describing the group as a cult of Far Right extremists and the charismatic leader has started going by a German name.

In 1992, it is discovered that Michael, in an ecstasy of fundraising, has accidentally defrauded several old women of their life savings.

In 1994, upon his release from prison, the boys, their wives, and children move to a pleasant suburb in Vancouver, Canada, where they become exceedingly successful capitalists in distantly related fields. Midge and Saul join them there and live happily into their nineties.

Midge leaves.

Aaron and Frieda.

A face-off.

Vibrating.

AARON: Mrs., um, Cohen.

FRIEDA (THRUSTS PAGES AT HIM): *Read.*

She hurries out.

AARON: It was the day we were moving to the other side of Levittown and we were very excited. Lou was at work so I was preparing the move myself. I was on a cigarette break with my friends Ruthie and Lenore.

RUTHIE: What can I pack?

FRIEDA: It's all packed. I did it all myself.

LENORE: Yourself!

FRIEDA: Listen, it was mostly diapers.

Ruthie, you remember Lenore, don't you, from the Sister-hood?

RUTHIE (VAGUELY): Sure.

FRIEDA: We passed out Hanukkah gelt together.

RUTHIE: Oh, of course!

LENORE: Nice to see you again.

RUTHIE: Good to see you again.

FRIEDA: The new place is a corner lot.
    I'm gonna have a real garden, like Italy—I'm so excited I can't tell you!

LENORE: But it's not gonna be all garden—you'll leave some grass for the baby to play in.

FRIEDA: Of course, what am I, a bad mother?

RUTHIE: Where *is* Toddy? I wanna give him a smooch.

    Pause.

FRIEDA: I don't know.

LENORE: No, really.

FRIEDA: He was here on the lawn—

LENORE: Go looking!

RUTHIE: Ask the neighbors!

FRIEDA: I've never even seen that woman; she's brand-new.
    Todd! Toddy!

LENORE: Todd!

RUTHIE: Todd!

The baby comes crawling; Frieda picks him up. Again, this can be a mime thing.

RUTHIE: He was next door.

LENORE: We should ask what happened.

FRIEDA: We should shut our mouths and continue.
This is not The Day I Lost the Baby.

RUTHIE: There are footprints on his diapers.

LENORE: He's been *kicked?*

FRIEDA: He's happy as a clam.
Don't tell Lou.

LENORE: But—

FRIEDA: I'm moving in seconds! We'll have all-new neighbors!
Now we go about the business of forgetting.

AARON: She doesn't take the writing class again.
The house next door to hers becomes available. She and her husband buy it, tear it down,
erect a greenhouse. The garden grows more famous than ever. She writes a column in a supermarket handout. It's called "Make Your Garden Grow Perfectly."
For several years in the early eighties, she returns to adult ed to teach Flower Arranging.

116

One Thanksgiving, after her husband dies, she's invited for dinner at the home—one town over—of her good, quiet son, Brian, who never said anything and had a sly smile and "knew things." After the meal, he gets her alone in the den.

FRIEDA: That was a good turkey.

She smiles.

Pause.

BRIAN: Why can't I point out France on a map?

She looks at him.

Why don't I know where France is? Or Romania? Or the Seychelles?

. . .

Why did I never learn the capitals of the states? Why do I have to look up which countries are in Central America and which are in South America?

Why don't I know a foreign language? Or quantum theory? Or trigonometry? Why did no one ever explain that math was beautiful when I was young and it might have made a difference?

Why don't I know the names of my great-grandparents or where they lived or if they died in some historical way?

Why, when I asked a question about them, did you always get tired?

Why, when I asked a question about *anything*, did you always get tired?

Why did you *have* me if I was going to be so fatiguing?

Why did you never realize that I had the potential to be something? To be a *person*, a citizen of the *world*?

Why did you never tell me that the world *applied* to me? What was the point of keeping that information from me? What was the point of keeping all information from me? What was the point of—of—

What was the point of—

What was the point?

ANNA: I'm sorry.

Brian looks on the verge of being grateful.

Have we been introduced?

He exits.

Anna comes in.

ANNA: I heard conversation—who were you talking to?

FRIEDA: Some guy, he wanted to know where France is, I don't know.

ANNA: . . . You having fun?

FRIEDA: Oh yes, the turkey was delicious.

They smile, exit.

Joan and Aaron alone.

JOAN: Well.

AARON: Well!

JOAN: Is this, then, liberation?

AARON: . . . I don't know if—

JOAN: Last day of school, first day of summer, baseball and ices—

AARON: I'm beyond that phase. Besides, it's winter.

JOAN: Liberation, then, from . . .
　　　　. . .
　　　　. . . ?

AARON: The commute began to—

JOAN: Once a week—

AARON: Still—

JOAN: Really, is that such a trial?

AARON: . . . No.

JOAN: What have you learned?

AARON: I'm the teacher.

JOAN: You are *not* a teacher.

AARON: Technically.

JOAN: That was a congratulation: You are not a teacher.
　　　　You resisted. You triumphed.
　　　　. . .
　　　　. . .

Though I have learned that there is no God. And the customs
that bind a community and omit me
are weak anyway
and therefore need not be lamented. Thank you for that.
. . .
. . .
. . .
There must be a later train.

AARON: No—

JOAN: Or one tomorrow.
Or one that goes in an opposite direction. There must be
something else.
. . .
I find tomorrow unimaginable.

Pause.

Don't be silent!
This silence! This silence when things finally matter! It always lets you win.

AARON: Joan.

JOAN: What keeps us from taking what we want?

Beat.

If there's no God
and customs are weak and affection has died
and our relatives don't weigh in . . .
. . .
where does this *restraint* come from?

AARON: My cab will . . . I have to go—

JOAN: To what? Why?

   . . .

   No: Go.

AARON: Um . . . yes—

JOAN: Stop!

AARON: Joan—

JOAN: Is the former Melissa Stanton Ames waiting with a bottle of celebratory Ripple and a worried look?

AARON: Actually, I told my parents I'd stop by.

JOAN: . . . You have parents?

AARON: Yes.

   . . . They live in Rockville Centre.

   Just a few stops over on the Babylon line, but I'm constantly neglecting them.

JOAN: You're *from* here?

AARON: Not . . . *here.* Not exactly, no.

   Well.

JOAN: I've tried every word trick I know.

   I've tried wooing and shaming and abracadabra and nothing's worked.

AARON: I'm really not worth the effort.

JOAN: You're the only one I can talk to.

AARON: Why?

JOAN: We're colleagues. You're a writer, too.

AARON (GLIBLY CYNICAL, NOT MEANING IT): Possibly a terrible one—

JOAN: That doesn't bother me!

>   *Beat.*

>   I'm so scared of going inside again.

AARON (TO US): Nothing will happen between us, not this night or any other. And she *will* go inside again.
>   Not completely.
>   She'll need to take jobs
>   to supplement the household income but there'll be a few more years of . . . fraught nothing,
>   of partial relapse.
>   Then her husband will be killed in a freak accident and there'll follow months
>   of near total silence,
>   broken only when the kitchen faucet erupts and she has to call in help from the outside.

>   *Joan is with a handyman.*

JOAN: I can't get it to stop.
>   I had to turn off the spout.

HANDYMAN: Uh-huh.

JOAN: If this were the city, I'd call the super.

HANDYMAN: Uh-huh.

JOAN: If my husband were alive—

HANDYMAN: You're a widow?

JOAN: Yes.

HANDYMAN: Huh. Young.

JOAN: Thank you.

HANDYMAN: He get hit by a bus or something?

JOAN: . . . Yes!

HANDYMAN: Huh!

JOAN: Yes!

HANDYMAN: Wow, I got that right. Cool.
> . . .
> So, wait.
> Are you the lady whose husband got hit by the bus?

JOAN: . . .
> Probably.

HANDYMAN: My mom told me.

JOAN: Your *mom*?

HANDYMAN: I think she knows you.

AARON: Because this is Todd Cohen Problem Child
    back from 'Nam and a handyman for the time being
    until he can think what to do with himself.

JOAN: Your mother's Frieda?

TODD: Yeah.

JOAN: We had a class together.

TODD: Yeah!

JOAN: She didn't care for me.

TODD: Nah.

AARON: This is that baby who crawled one day into her living room
    with the force of an omen and whom she booted out.
    She'll never put the two together.

JOAN: What was it like, Vietnam? What a stupid question! "What was
    it like, Viet..."

TODD: It was a green belt of death.

    Beat.

JOAN: Who said that?

TODD: Me.

JOAN: Who said it before you?

TODD: I dunno. God, maybe.

> *Beat.*

> I didn't see combat, really. I didn't get hurt.
> I'm smart or test well or something so they gave me a type-
> writer
>   and made me useless. But around me, the kids, the stupid
> kids,
>   they were just . . . wham, smithereens, right? So I've been
> mostly . . .
>   Nights this has been mostly . . .
>   I lie awake
>   and try to figure it out, you know,
>   I try to put words to it
>   and that's what I thought last night: It was a "green belt of
> death."

JOAN: That's beautiful.

TODD: Is it?
>   I think it's a little forced.

JOAN: Your mother and I met in a class four years ago.
>   It's starting again next week. I thought I might . . .

> *They look at each other.*

AARON: They come to me together.

I am still reverse-commuting to Levittown. I have made progress: from sour to bitter.

Oh, hello.

JOAN: I'd heard you were still—

AARON: I, yes, am.

And you . . . still live here.

JOAN: Yes.

AARON: And your husband?

JOAN: Dead.

AARON: I'm sorry.

How did— He was still a youngish man, wasn't—

Husband appears.

HUSBAND: I can no longer bear your annihilating gaze.

JOAN: And I can no longer bear a grown man who is afraid of Manhattan Island.

HUSBAND: Is that what you think? I'll show you!

JOAN: So he took the train, Wantagh to Penn Station. And once he got there, I think he panicked.

I think he must have had a panic attack because when they found him he was dehydrated; he had perspired himself dry.

For solace, I think, he found the nearest hardware store. There he bought some wing nuts and a T square.

Then, the clerk said, he sauntered out of the store like a prizefighter who'd won his bout, and walked into the face of a moving bus.

AARON: I'm sorry.

JOAN: Why be?

He ended in triumph. And I don't miss him.

AARON: The Introduction:

JOAN: This young man is Todd Cohen.

He's taking the class, too.

AARON: Nice to meet you.

JOAN: Todd is the son of Frieda Cohen.

AARON: . . . Okay.

JOAN: She was in my class.

Aaron. Mystified.

My nemesis.

AARON: Oh! Yes!

I hope your mother's well.

TODD: She's, you know: Frieda.

JOAN: Todd has returned from Vietnam.

He has a story to tell.

AARON: Don't we all?

Lights.

But Todd did.

To get away from his mother, Todd worked in libraries,
the East Meadow library, which was the good one. Or at
Joan's house.

*He sits in Joan's chair. She kneels behind him, an arm
flung around him.*

And this happened.

They kiss. Then return to Todd's writing.

Then quickly, these things happened: They finished the
book.

Joan was coauthor. In her numb years, she read incessantly
and wrote covertly.

She was talented.

She was a gifted autodidact. By the time Todd came to her,
she could teach.

She was a *real* teacher.

The book was good.

The book was published.

The book was acclaimed.

The book made them a fortune.

The story of a noncombatant's experience in an undeclared
war. Todd was notably terse.

He was also notably good-looking. The two of them.

The book was made into a movie—Todd was given a TV deal. His series was a hit.

One day, he visited me.

TODD: Aaron.

AARON: My God.

TODD: Todd Cohen.

AARON: Yes, of course I—

TODD: Listen, I read your story.

AARON: What story?

TODD: In the *Sewanee Review.*

AARON: That was published in the Pleistocene age—

TODD: Made me cry, man.

AARON: Oh!

TODD: Left me in a puddle.

AARON: Wow.

TODD: So, listen:
   I've got this TV thing. I've got this series.

And we're staffing.

And I was wondering if you're interested.

AARON: Pardon?

TODD: Would you like to *write* for it? You'd have to move to L.A.

AARON: And it turned out

I had a knack for this.

I suppose shunning a thing can give you a mastery of it. And my wife came with me.

In recent years I had taken to listing her flaws on a ruled notepad.

Flaw: Believes in me absolutely despite the copious evidence that this is an empty belief; thus, she's an ignoramus.

Flaw: Dresses shabbily in the clothes I can afford to buy for her.

Flaw: Will only take jobs that pay less than mine do in a crass effort to protect what she doubtless thinks of as my "male ego."

Flaw: Enjoys reading novels by first-time writers.

Flaw: Is perpetually blameless, faithful, kindhearted, and uncomplaining, making separation impossible.

But in L.A., I found myself crossing off these flaws one by one until one day I saw that they'd all been eliminated and deduced that I loved her again

—no—that's not how it happened.

I admitted that I always had loved her

and what we'd needed had never been a change of people— just of circumstances.

One day I'm in New York for Christmas:

Joan and a woman walk by.

Joan?

130

JOAN: Oh my God!

AARON: Hi!

They hug.

JOAN: Aaron—Aaron Port.
What are you doing—

AARON: Home for Christmas. You?

JOAN: I live here.
Well.
And I'm on my way to see my publisher. "My publisher"!
What a thing!

AARON: You're publishing another—

JOAN: Yes. Yes!

AARON: Not with Todd, though—

JOAN: Oh God, no. We're—

AARON: I thought so—

JOAN: Not in years—

AARON: I didn't think—

JOAN: This is my friend Ramona—

AARON: Hello.

RAMONA: Pleased to meet you.

JOAN: Ramona is my very *good* friend.

AARON: Pleased to . . .

Pause.

So tell me about your book.

JOAN: Oh my God, it's a collection of my *pensées.*

AARON: I didn't know you were so influenced by Descartes—

JOAN: All that crap I used to throw into boxes—

AARON: It would go on to enormous success—one of the many minor "signal works" of those years—it's never gone out of print.

JOAN: Who knows if two people will buy it but it makes me happy.

AARON: That's great.

To us:

She would publish other books, none as successful as the first, but the first would turn out to be enough.

She was a figure. She lasted.

In the eighties, there were a few noted romances, a brief but splashy marriage to a venture capitalist.

About twenty years ago, she retired to Wellfleet, where she lived quietly.

She still does, I think—at least if she died, I'm sure I'd have heard about it.

Back to Joan:

Listen: I'm late to meet my wife—

JOAN: Are you still married to that same wife?

AARON: Yes.

JOAN (WITH ENORMOUS COMPASSION): Oh.

AARON: I didn't have time to correct her.
        Nice meeting you, Ramona.
        Good to see you again, Joan.
        Good-bye.

JOAN (STOPPING HIM): Aaron! Thank you.

AARON: For what?

JOAN: Since I met you . . . It's all been so interesting.

AARON: But I digress.
        In fact I've been digressing for the last twenty minutes.
        It happens at this age—you tell yourself
        it *won't* but—you have so much information, you want to say
    everything, it's very hard to stick to the point.
        So.
        Forget all that stuff.
        And now let's return to the end of the story proper—the one
    I meant to be telling—which,
        if you remember, is an account of events

that took place over a few months in late fall and early winter of 1967.

Lights.

JOAN: I'm so scared of going inside again.

AARON: You won't.

JOAN: You're sure of that, are you?

AARON (WITHOUT CONVICTION): Yes.

> *They stand there, lost.*

I don't know what's stopping me but something is.
I'm sorry.

JOAN (MORE SORRY THAN ATTACKING): You're a disgrace.

AARON: Maybe so.

JOAN (STOPPING HIM FROM GOING): You have to listen to my story.

AARON: What?

JOAN: My last piece for the class. You have to hear it; it's your duty.

AARON: I—

JOAN: Here it is:

> . . .
> Once upon a time

a girl came from the sticks who was witty and unread and
she met a man
    who seemed like a poet because she was unread
    and didn't know he was a plagiarist.
    . . .

    . . .

So they moved to a house that was almost new
    and far too small
    and where the man twiddled his thumbs and took out a pat-
ent on it.
    And in this manner decades passed.
    It turned out
    she was in a trance until one day
    she woke up and met a man
    who called himself a teacher,
    though he refused to teach
    and did teach though he didn't mean to.
    And she thought of him nightly and pictured him naked
    and so did he her.
    He was a firebrand who
    like all the scriveners of his generation believed in silence
cunning exile
    but in him it was starting to turn to sadness curdling exhaus-
tion.
    They had come to live
    or, in his case, spend several hours a week
    in a place that had fallen out of the precincts of history and
prided itself on that.
    But these two believed tacitly
    that they might reenter with a kiss
    that would smash up everything.

They came to the last moment when that would be possible and she waited.

Because though she did not scruple against making this move herself she knew it would change nothing

unless it came from him.

A moment.

AARON: Good night, Joan.

He leaves.

JOAN: He declined.

And she returned home.

And nothing ever happened to her again.

She goes to the door.

The End.

She shuts the lights. End of play.

Printed in the United States
by Baker & Taylor Publisher Services

Printed in the United States
by Baker & Taylor Publisher Services